CE

# VIRGIL

# VIRGIL

**HASKELL HOUSE PUBLISHERS Ltd.**

*Publishers of Scarce Scholarly Books*

**NEW YORK, N. Y. 10012**

**1972**

**HASKELL HOUSE PUBLISHERS** LTD.

*Publishers of Scarce Scholarly Books*

280 LAFAYETTE STREET

NEW YORK, N. Y. 10012

Library of Congress Cataloging in Publication Data

Woodberry, George Edward, 1855-1930.
  Virgil.

  1. Vergilius Maro, Publius.  I.  Title.
PA6826.W6  1972            871'.01            72-3495
ISBN 0-8383-1564-X

Printed in the United States of America

# FOREWORD

*Scholarly and literary societies the world over have been asked to take part in honoring the bi-millennial of Virgil. The Authors Club, as its reply to the invitation, immediately decided to publish in book form the greatest of essays on Virgil ever written by an American scholar. Messrs. Harcourt, Brace and Company, publishers of Professor Woodberry's volume wherein the Virgil essay forms one of a noble group, gladly gave their consent; the Woodberry Society was equally willing, and Professor Woodberry wrote: "It is a very high honor that you propose, on the part of the Committee of The Authors Club, should it publish the little book you suggest, and, for my part, I should welcome the distinction, only feeling that it is too little deserved. The essay has never been reprinted, and it has had kind words from Latin scholars, as well as from friends."*

It has had far more than that. Lovers of literature and widely known critics regard Professor Woodberry's "Virgil," because of the profundity of its interpretation, the universal content of its philosophy, and the rare beauty of its language, as one of those writings which, critical in inception, belong to the realm of creative literature.

     ❀     ❀     ❀     ❀     ❀     ❀     ❀     ❀

These prefatory lines were written before Mr. Woodberry's death on January the second, 1930. In our sorrow, this book becomes in a sense a memorial to him as well as to the ancient poet whom he loved.

GEORGE S. HELLMAN, Chairman

GEORGE M. WHICHER

JOHN ERSKINE, Ex Officio

*Committee on Publication*

**VIRGIL**

is that poet whose verse has had most power in the world. He was
the poet of Rome, and concentrated in his genius its imperial star;
so long as that ruled the old Mediterranean world, with the great
northwest and eastern hinterlands, Virgil summed its glory for the
human populations that fleeted away in that vast basin; in a world

forever mightily changing his solitary pre-eminence was one un-changing thing, dimmed only as the empire itself faded. His memory illumined the Dark Ages. He rose again as the morning star of the Latin races. He penetrated the reborn culture of Europe with the persistency and pervasiveness of Latinity itself; not only was knowledge of his works as wide-spread as education, but his influence on the artistic temperament of literatures, the style of authors and even the characters of men in their comprehension of the largeness of life, was subtle and profound, and was the more ample in proportion to the nearness of the new nations to the direct descent of civilization. He, more than any other poet, has been a part of the intellectual life of Europe alike by length of sway and by the multitude of minds he touched in all generations; and, among the Latin races, he is still the climax of their genius, for charm and dignity, for art and the profound substance of his matter, and for its serious inclusiveness of human life. Of no other poet can it be said that his lines are a part of the biography of the great, of emperors like Augustus and Hadrian, of fathers like Jerome and Augustine, of preachers like Savonarola, churchmen like Fenelon, statesmen like Pitt and Burke; and among the host of humble scholars, of schoolmasters, the power he has held in their bosoms is as remarkable for its personal intimacy as for its universal embrace. No fame so majestic has been cherished with a love so tender. Virgil thus blends in a marvelous manner the authority of a classic with the direct appeal to life.

It belongs to the sense of familiar companionship which Virgil's verse exhales that some shadows of his personality survive, slight but sufficient for memory and affection. He was the son of a small farmer, in the province of North Italy, of whom no more is known than that he wished to give his child the best education then to be had. We first see him, who was to be so great a poet, as the slender tall schoolboy at Cremona and Milan, with the rusticity of manner which he never laid aside. He studied also at Rome, in his youth, and found patrician friends among his mates. He made his way later with men of great affairs, and notwithstanding the shyness of his heart and the awkwardness of his manners they found something to prize in him by some charm the Muses shed, loved him, petted and praised him, and gave him a fortune, a house at Rome, near Mæcenas' garden, which he seldom used, and two country homes at Naples and Nola, where he loved to live in the soft Campanian air; there, except for sojourns in Sicily and pleasant travel in the Greek cities and along the islands, he passed those meditative years of privacy in which his self-distrustful and long-brooding genius slowly matured its eternal work; there, too, as he desired, at Naples, over by the hill of Posilipo, his ashes were laid to rest in that pleasant city's soil, which still keeps the tradition of his tomb. He was happy in the protecting affection of his friends, and also in the honor of the world which rose to him as to Augustus when he entered the theater, and in the power of lifelong labor in his art undiminished by an hour wasted on inferior things. In all outward ways his life was the most fortunate recorded in literature; and it is good to know that the world was gentle to one of those delicate spirits who, usually with how different a fate, bring it gifts from eternity. In the memory of Virgil there is no bitterness of regret for the words of unkindness or the blows of adversity; he lived peacefully and in the habitual enjoyment of some of the fairest gifts of life.

Nowhere so much as in those works which seem most independent of the power of time, which escape from their own age, their native country and race, and enter upon a cycle of memory so vast that they are fitly named the stars of the intellectual firmament, is it needful to define their moment, to understand the nest of their conception, the law of their creation, the nature of their first appeal to men, in a word their contemporaneity. The moment of Virgil is declared plainly in the *Eclogues*. They are little poems, the labored trifles of his 'prentice hand; but in them, like the oak in the acorn there is in miniature all Virgil; both the man and his work are there like a preconception. The teachableness of Virgil is his prime character, and shines in his youth. He woke to the past as simply as a child opens its eyes to the dancing sunlight of the world, and he took it in directly as something belonging to him. He made speed to enter on his inheritance; and for him this heritage in its special form was the glory of Greek literature. The imaginative interpretation of the world stored in a thousand years of Greek poetry was the food of his heart. Thus it came about that he did not begin to write in a way discovered and worked out merely by himself, but imitated, as it is said, Theocritus the Syracusan, the chief Greek master of pastoral verse. He could not have had better fortune. For a youth unacquainted with experience the artificial

mode of life which the pastoral presents as its framework of inci-
dent and song is itself favorable, since its requirements of accurate
representation of reality are less stringent; and, especially, its small
scale enforces attention to detail and encourages perfection of
phrase, line and image in the workmanship and condensation in
the matter, while its variety of description, dialogue and inserted
song and its blend of lyric and dramatic moods give scope to a
mind experimenting as it learns. It is for this reason that so many
of the world's great poets in their youth have tried their wings in
these numbers, brief, composite, academic, so well fitted for the
exercise of growing talents, already touched with scholarship, in a
world not too real to be lightly held nor so fantastic as to preclude
truth of feeling. Virgil derived the proper good from the imitation of
a great master by developing through it his native power. Theocritus
remained the master-singer of the idyl; but before the different
genius of Virgil passed on to its own toils, he had left the sweetness
of his youth here in the pastoral like a perfume forever.

The poetic life of Virgil, however, in these years was more pro-
found than this. He was not merely training his genius in certain
external modes of expression; he was unfolding his soul. Form was
the Greek gift to Virgil; not only that form which exists in the outer
structure of line and melody or within the verse in its logic of emo-
tion and event, but form which has power to cast the mind itself in
predetermined lines of feeling and action, of taste, of choice, of
temperament, and finds utterance in that beauty of the soul which
is precedent to all verse. Form in its religious moods has this power

to possess and shape the souls of men, as is familiarly seen; and so artistic form, alive and bodied in the lovely and ancient Greek tradition, seized Virgil in the spirit and fashioned him; he was its child as the novice is the spiritual son of St. Francis. The opposition between Theocritus and Virgil lies in this: in Theocritus, life puts on the forms of art; in Virgil art puts on the forms of life. In the Syracusan idyls there is objective beauty—pictures idealized and detached from life; in the Mantuan *Eclogues* one feels rather the presence of a beautiful soul to which art has given the gift of tongues to speak to all men. This deep intimate compelling mastery of the Greek spirit over all that was artistic in Virgil shaped him almost in his essential being; he was Hellenized as by a second birth. It was characteristic of him to yield to the will of life, and he yielded happily to the Greek forms of imagination, for he found in this obedience that yoke in which alone everlasting freedoms lie and the power of a free soul; it released his personality as if by some divine and creative touch. This presence of Virgil in his verse is elementary. He was a lover, and through love disengaged from life its moment of beauty, of sentiment, of millennial hope; but this beauty, sentiment and hope are seen under that almost atmospheric charm which has coined for itself the name Virgilian and is breathed from himself. It is not for what these eclogues contain of Theocritus that they have been dear to the poets of all lands, any more than it is for what the youthful lines of Spenser and Milton contain of these eclogues that the English breathings of the pastoral are dear; it is because they express with great purity and sweetness the genius of Virgil in its tender age.

If any one finds in the eclogues only the echo of Theocritus, he is wide of the mark; his ear is not set to the ringing of the master-melody in their song. The poets used the same instrument, and the younger learned its use from the elder; but each employed it with a difference, and this difference is a gulf of ages between them and an opposition in the spring and impulse of poetry. Art is not life, but is evoked from life. Theocritus held the mirror to life, but its image in his verse though more beautiful is still a thing of the external world; he stands outside what he depicts and renders it for its own sake. Virgil projected himself into life, and is the center of the world he expresses; he uses it to illustrate his own personality, to body forth his own various loves of beauty, nature, sentiment, romance, aspiration, to clothe with the forms of life that soul which art had shaped in him. He was still, though thirty, only a half-boyish lover of books and nature and a few friends, and the world he lived in was but little known to him; the eclogues with the personality of autobiography disclose this young scholar in his world. Virgil's world, too, like the temperamental drift of his art, is different from that of Theocritus; it is one more diversified, more actual and contemporaneous even; it is a Roman, Italian, proconsular world. He thinks of Actium and Parthia as we to-day think of Santiago and the Philippines. His landscape has the face and pro-file of familiar haunts; his shepherds have the features of his own rustics; his interests are his own local and temporal affairs. The pastoral Arcadia is a convention by means of which the encum-brances of time and place and persons and much matter of fact are gotten rid of; but under its clear veil which softens the unimportant, stand undisguised the men and events, the sentiment, the friendships, the scenes, the recreations, all the loves of the young poet from the humblest and tenderest up to the hope of all the world which he in those first years sounded for eternal memory as none before or since has sung the strain. Such is the Roman substance, personal, Italian, imperial, of it all, notwithstanding the superficial artifice of the poetic form.

Roman, too, was the seriousness of the young poet in his art. He and his fellow poets of the age were in literature provincials whose metropolis was Greek letters. They set themselves to the patriotic task of bringing the Greek muses to Latium where Æneas had brought the Trojan gods, and creating in Latin something as near the Greek poetry as they could accomplish, and by very obviously, often direct, imitative means. They were zealous in the work; all were serious in it, however light the touch or the topic they strove to transplant to their own language and world. Virgil was such a provincial, though Greek art was itself refined in passing through his temperament; and he had such seriousness of mind. To compare great things with small, he was not unlike the young Longfellow in America who was avid of all the literatures of Europe and assimilated the poetic tradition of the thousand years preceding his birth, and who also strove with like seriousness to compass something like that in his own new land; and like Virgil, he too, in after life created for his country its native romance and primitive sentiment, giving to its desert nakedness an ascribed and imputed poetry. The Roman moment, also, in the largest way, was not unlike our own. Virgil was born in a dawning age; for him, as for us, life had been long lived in the world, there was antiquity, the thousand years of literature, and vanishing religions; Egypt was, perhaps, even more a monument of the Unknown Death than to-day; but with the spread of the power of Rome, which was then what the spread of liberty now is, a new age was at hand. Law and peace, which were the other names of Rome, had the world in their grasp, and were conquering far outward along its dark barbaric edges even to Britain "sundered once from all the human race." It was then that Virgil, "in the foremost files of time," sang in his youth that eclogue, the *Pollio* which is the greatest hymn of antiquity, if not of all time, and won for himself, though a pagan, a place among the saints of the Church:

*Magnus ab integro saeclorum nascitur ordo.*

The line has the swell of the *Gloria*. Thus early, thus fundamental by virtue of its earliness, arose in him and mingled with his genius that temperament of world-hope, not the diminutive Arcadian dream of a valley or distant islands of the blessed, but world-hope mighty as the world, on the great scale of universal sympathy for mankind, which was one of the authentic signs of a new time. It was the secular hour of the founding of the Empire; it was the spiritual hour of the birth of Christ; and its presence was in the young poet's heart. A mighty voice, too, had before now been heard in Rome, the voice of one crying in the wilderness of the dethroned gods, a man so great that he could endure the longest probation of any of the poets of mankind and wait nineteen centuries for the fullness of his fame—Lucretius. Virgil heard the voice, and stored it in his heart, and meditated upon it; but the time was not yet come. It was the eve of a great past, the dawn of a great future; and the further one penetrates the verse, the more clearly stands out this youthful figure with the radiance of the world's new morning in his face.

The *Eclogues*, obeying the law of all beautiful things, have gathered beauty from the lapse of time. Some light streams back upon them from the later glory of Virgil, and they have that increase of charm which belongs to things that have been long loved; the lines, too, like shells, are full of vocal memories. For one who knows them well and knows the poets, they are a nest of the singing birds of all lands; as he reads, voices of Italy, France and England blend with the familiar lines, and a choiring vision rises before him of the world's poets in their youth framing their lips to the smooth-sliding syllables; for the eclogues have been deeply cherished. They are loved chiefly, however, because the young Virgil is seen in them, as in the palæstra of his art before he had put on his singing-robes, with that sweet teachableness, that yielding and hospitable mind, out of which was to come, to bless him and the world, the wide receptivity of his spirit, the rich assimilation, the accumulated power of imagination in the race, already held in the grasp of his genius like Ithuriel's spear. Rome and Athens, the light and majesty of the world, were married in his blood; and though he bore as yet only the rustic reed, here in the adolescence of genius was the form of him

who was to hand down by descent the antique vigor to the modern
world. Virgil became the great reconciler in his own inherited
world, the great mediator between antiquity and Christendom; he
maintained in poetry, equally with Plato in philosophy, the un-
broken continuity of the human spirit; but before entering on these
great offices and preliminary to them he was first of all and by in-
stinct a great lover—a greater lover than Dante—and here in the
first friendly affections of the senses melting with the world, of the
heart blending with other lives, of the mind breathing the univer-
sal hope of all, is this lover in the bud—he, who was to be the greatest
lover in all the world of all things beautiful, strong, tender, pitiful,
sad, and fated.

There was another scope, a different fiber, in the *Georgics,* the
fruit of his seven years' toil in early manhood. His genius had been
powerfully condensed; the matter of the song was as firmly organ-
ized as it was richly diversified; the whole, scarcely two thousand
lines in all, was a great single poem. The sense of nationality, no
longer diffused and dispersed, burns at the center as its nucleus and
feeding flame. The work, though small in scale is monumental in
effect; it bears the Roman birthmark in its practical purpose to
share in the restoration of the agricultural life, and in the author's
dedication of his powers to public spirit. It was characteristic of
Virgil to require reality in his subject-matter, and a present hour;
contemporaneousness presided in the inception and purpose of all
he did; however far he might range, he brought all home to amplify
that moment of Rome in which he lived. More than any other of

the poets of mankind he used the poetic art to idealize, to exalt and to enrich the nation's consciousness; and, through singleness of mind and comprehensiveness of effort, he became the most national of all poets. As the world had been given to Rome to rule, Rome had been given to him to be the Empire of his song; this was his destiny. His genius did not expand suddenly and at once to so vast a sphere; but as is the case with all men who accumulate greatness as if by a process of nature, humbler impulses and lesser tasks conducted him upon his way. He would tell the story of Italy—that was the phase under which Rome first appealed to him. It was as if some one of our own poets had chosen to write an idyl of the old free life of New England, in the days before national unity and American destiny had come to fullness in his heart. With unerring instinct, in choosing his theme, he struck straight at the fundamental Roman interest, the land, the soil; but not yet imperializing, he seized this interest not in its foreign form of land-hunger which is the impulse of all empire, but in its primitive form of the home-domain, "the mighty mother of men and fruits," that Italy which was Rome's birthright. He thought of the land, too, not as our nature-poets do in modern days as a description of contour and color and changes of the weather, the magic of the senses, but primitively as the dwelling place of the race and the element of its labors. Toil; that, too, was a Roman idea, and he yoked it with the land in a Roman way; for he saw human life on the soil as an arduous and unremitting warfare with the stubborn obduracy of nature, who being subdued, nevertheless, became beneficent, rejoicing in her captivity, and rewarded her conqueror with the harvest of the earth and its loveliness, with the external blessings of the gods and with moral boons of inward excellence stored in the characters of men by this discipline of the perennial task of life.

The *Georgics* is the story of this perennial task. In its original and parent form no more than an almanac, a manual of the planting of crops, the raising of cattle and the tending of bees, it grew in Virgil's mind to be a poem of the sacred year. Virgil was by instinct and temperament a ritualist. The regularity inherent in times and seasons and all ceremonial, the solemnity belonging to all rites, the presence of the abstract and hidden in their significance, were things profoundly Roman and responded to what was by race deeply implanted in his nature. The round of the seasons in their connection with agricultural life was in his eyes a ritual of the year, the presence and action of a natural religion. The dependence of man on nature always plays a great part in religious life; even now when that dependence is less definitely felt than in primitive times it is at birth, marriage and death, the great moments of nature, that religion has its common and vital impact on the general life; and in the primitive conditions, set forth in this poem, nature might seem herself to appoint the sacred days of the gods both for prayer and for thanksgiving, to order the festivals in their course and to prescribe the peculiar service for the hour, month after month, in annual revolution. The needs of each season and the pursuits appropriate to it determined the active duties of man, and these drew after them the due religious practices consecrated by use and wont; and, in the issue of all, the blessings of the divine gods crowned the labor with a present reward. Natural piety could not have a simpler being than this. The mystery of the world which envelops all life-processes on the earth has always overhung the out-of-doors people with some grandeur in the elements, with stars and winds and waves; in living near to nature, they seem, by virtue of being lost and unprotected there, to reach out to the unknown in habitual ways. Virgil felt this mystery after a different fashion; he knew it in the forms of old mythology that Greek imagination had put on in the divine presence, and also in the forms of new science that Greek intellect had put forth in attempting a rational conception of nature as a thing subject to human knowledge. He was not disturbed by this double possession of imagination and rational intuition; that teachable, that yielding and hospitable mind, by its own nature made him in his self-expression a representative poet; he gave out life in its wholeness. This sacred year, with its ritual of work and worship, drew his eyes upon it, as a thing of outward beauty, and first gave up to his gaze, first of men, that enveloping charm of the land and its life which is now the world's thought of Italy; this year, too, with its antique usages, as old, perhaps, as the tilled soil itself, recurring in their seasons as the sun rose in the zodiac, engaged his affections by which he was bound to all things of reverence, age and piety, and none more than he realized in his heart both their divine and human appeal; and, with all this, awoke, too, the philosophic mind, fed from later fountains, and he flung round this ancient Italy, humanized by long life upon its soil, that large horizon of the intellect, in which his own time was beginning to live.

In such ways as these the poem which was begun as a manual of the farm's task-work came from Virgil's hands so touched with visible beauty, old religious association, the mythology and science of the Mediterranean world and his own loves for all these, that it was, without fiction, an incarnate Italy. He had embodied in his verse the land itself with all its loveliness, then as it is to-day, a land long lived in, with history, legend and ruins of a storied past reaching back into the unknown ages; he had set forth its characteristic life, the human product of the soil, as a thing so sharing in the simplicities of nature and what is divinely primitive as to make it seem the eternal model of what the life of man on earth should be, under the dispensation of labor, yet enveloped in the kindly agencies of sun and rain, springtide and summer heat and mellowing falls, the birth and rebirth of all things in the revolution of the year—a life which was itself religion, a round of duty, prayer and praise; and he had evoked from this land and the life there lived in the plains and uplands that abstract Italy, the eldest of the modern nations, in unveiling whom he may almost be said to have created the mother-land. It is the same Italy, then and now; the stream of Italian patriotism still mounts to the hymn of the second Georgic as its fountain-head. There Italy is first seen clothed with the divinity that a land identified with a race and a renown takes on in the hearts of its children. Virgil seized the fact in its moment, with that revelation of the actual which the highest poetry exists to achieve. He sees Italy as the center of the world, with other lands antique or barbarous lying on the sea about and beyond her, each with its just distance and coloring and place in the Mediterranean world, which is her sphere, but subject and tributary to her unenvious supremacy in fertility and men and fame. The miracle is the perfection with which Virgil expresses this security in happiness, beauty and power, this unclouded felicity of fortune, this ordered peace, while distant clouds of war and menace whirl only on the far confines of the scene.

He had prepared himself with wonderful thoroughness for the work; a broad base of scholarship lies under it, and for the didactic substance he had brought all Greek and Roman knowledge, and something even from Carthage, to contribute to its truth, precision and fullness; but it was rather by his cultural knowledge, which he used in heightening and expanding the theme to its true proportions, that he regenerated and transformed the matter of the verse and made the rural scene into the glory of Italy. The wealth of this preparation, and his seven years' toil, may seem disproportionate to the result in a poem so brief, but only to those who do not know that, the scale of the matter being allowed for, the power of a poem is in inverse proportion to its length. He used for his artistic method a selective, partial description, subordinating individuality and detail to social and general presentation, and he employed episode, suggestion and the emphasis that lies in enthusiasm to enlarge the theme and qualify it with greatness; in particular, he intended no exhaustion of the subject but only of

the feeling of the subject, which is the method of great poetry, and
hence come the rapidity, the variety, the completeness of impres-
sion which are the most obvious traits of the changeful lines. The
*Georgics,* most of all, reveals the master of the poetic art; and in
a work somewhat limited by its choice of one, though a great and
enduring, phase of human life and also by its national inspiration
and its attachment to a particular social moment, the mind has
leisure to notice the more its artistic modes, the choice and order-
ing of the material, the colors of rhetoric, the edge and immobility
of style ever fresh and everlasting as sculpture, the wealth of
mosaic, the pictorial, sententious and eclectic compositeness, the
elaboration of the poem's beauty in the whole and in detail. It is
full of a poet's choices; and, though popular with the cultivated
class to which it was addressed, is essentially a poet's poem. True
to himself, the stuff which Virgil worked in was his own nature;
out of his heart brooding on the beauty of the visible world about
him, on the picture of its human labors and the imperial care con-
serving all these things in happy and lasting peace, came the vision
shaped and colored and idealized by his sympathies with man's life,
his affections for the things of old time, his hopes in the present. The
*Georgics* in a land of patriots and poets is still the unrivaled monu-
ment of the first poet-lover of Italy.

The *Æneid,* Virgil's last and greatest work, is a world-poem.
It is one of that splendid cluster of world-poems, which by the
fewness of their number, the singleness of their glory, and the great
intervals of time that separate them, have, of all man's works,

most infinitude; though time attacks them, they survive like the pyramids; they are man's Bibles on the side that he turns to the human, like the Scriptures on the side that he turns to the divine. The distinctive feature of the *Æneid* is the arc of time it covers, the burden of time it supports. After that song of Italy, of the land and the life, the genius of Virgil struck a deeper compass of reality and seized the theme at its heart. "Utter my toiling power," said Rome. The tale of the wanderings of Æneas and how he brought the Trojan gods to Latium is only the fable; over and beyond all the character and event which it contains, and including these like an atmosphere, it is a symbol of the massive labor of the seven centuries that had for their crown and climax the pacified Augustan world.

*Tantae molis erat Romanam condere gentem.*

This massive labor, this toiling power, is the theme. It is not the Homeric world; no ten years' foray, brilliant with Greek personality, in the dawn of history; no passionate boy, though the most splendid of all Alexanders, great in his sulking wrath, his comrade-love and his battle-glory; no chieftains parleying in the council and warriors rushing in the field; not these. It is the Virgilian world —Rome at the summit of her Empire, rising from those seven centuries of interminable strain. Rome in the verse is its creative impulse, and governs the poem in its whole and in its parts. The sense of past time, too, always so strong in Virgil, is never relaxed. The *Æneid* is the book of an old world.

Æneas is, in his character, Rome concentrated—a man set against the world; and in him, too, is that perspective of the past. He has outlived his personal life; his city is in ashes, his wife is dead; there remains nothing for himself, only to live for others, to obey the will of the gods, devotion to a public end. He is characterized by patience which alike to the Pagan and the Christian world, to the Oriental and the Occidental mind, is the greatest virtue of man, and was the state virtue of Rome; to endure, however distant the goal, however frequent the defeat, however adverse men and fortune and the gods. The *Æneid* is the book of victory deferred, as imperial Rome, to one looking backward on her past, was the last fruit of time, the late issue of long and perilous struggle through generations. Toil, which in the song of Italy was linked with the land, is here fused with the power of empire; but it is toil—the same Roman idea, though more informed with grandeur, and it draws with it the same rule of life, obedience, though more set forth with the stern absoluteness that belonged to Roman discipline. If Æneas offends romantic sentiment by deserting Dido at Carthage, he conformed thereby to the Roman ideal of right in some of its deepest foundations; and even in the modern view, it may be suspected that if in place of the wing-heeled Mercury there had been some Hebrew prophet rebuking an erring David, the sympathy of the reader might run truer with the thoughts of Virgil. Rome would not tolerate the noblest of Antonys forgetting empire in passion for a woman; and Æneas, in abandoning Dido, was the reverse of Antony, and measured to the Roman rule of life. Æneas gains, and is truly seen, in proportion as the mind is free from the allurements of individuality, free from the worship of the ungovernable human power in life, and all that makes against the ideal of patience, obedience and rule; the grandeur of the individual is found in Mezentius and Turnus, creatures of self-will opposed to the will of heaven, and herein justly doomed to perish; if these latter seem the true heroes, it is as Satan is sometimes, and perhaps popularly, regarded as the hero of Milton, but to Milton Satan was infernal as to Virgil Turnus was impious. Æneas stands at the opposite pole of conduct; and if he shares the defective attraction which the typical Roman character historically discloses, he the more illustrates that efficient power in life, of which the sense greatens as time clarifies the mind of the ardors of youth, whether in men or nations; for the ideal implanted in him, like every part of the poem, bears the mark of a world grown old.

The presence of Roman time in the verse, especially the sense of the sorrows that are the price of empire, is also profoundly felt in the diffusion of pathos through the poem, not the pathos of individual lives but of the general lot, which makes it the saddest book of the world. It contains three great defeats: the destruction of Troy, the fall of Carthage, which is the atmosphere of fate in which the personal tragedy of Dido burns out on her funeral pyre, and the overthrow of Turnus; the true action is contained in these passages; and, in addition, though Æneas is finally successful, his checks have been so many and his success is so long delayed and is so palely realized that his career, in the impression it makes, may almost count as a fourth defeat. Against this scene of disaster the

majesty of Rome's final triumph in history, though it fills all the
horizons of the poem, blazes in vain. Here are the tears of time.
*Lacrymae rerum* seems almost the other name of the *Æneid,* as it
is its best known and central phrase. The "chanter of the Pollio"
had come to this. He who was the first to sound the strain of
world-hope was also now the first to strike that parallel chord of
world-woe which has reverberated down all after ages. The *Miserere*
follows the *Gloria* as manhood follows youth. If the *Æneid* were
only a poem of heroic action, and not a symbol of life long lived,
the suffering would be absorbed in the action; but the poem is
heavy with thought and clouded with feeling like a sun struggling
with eclipse. The intellectual force in it, the passion of thought,
Virgil's overmastering sympathy with the victim—and Æneas by
his long sufferings is essentially a victim—shake its containing
bounds, and again and again threaten its epical form. A thousand
lines have the lyrical cry; they could, and do, stand alone, each one
a poem. The dramatic power in the episode of Dido threatens to
overbear the moral unity of the structure; the didactic depth of
teaching in the descent to Hades threatens to intermit the sense
of action and shift the scene to the academy; and at every turn,
when the epic seems slipping from his hand, Virgil invokes Rome,
returns to that ground-swell of his music, and fuses all disparate
elements in its enveloping power. It is the thought of Ascanius and
the Julian line that overrules the wrongs of Dido; and in the Elysian
fields it is the encomium of Rome—the most majestic lines ever
written by the hand of man—and the bead-roll of her heroes and

the vision of her Augustan triumph that restore the epical interest and supremacy. It is in these ways most truly that, as Tennyson said, this "ocean-roll of rhythm sounds forever of imperial Rome."

Rome, too, sustains the verse in its weakest part, the mythology, and gives to that debilitated supernatural element the only reality which it contains. Virgil was born too late to be a true believer in Olympus; but in placing the prophecy of Rome on the lips of Jupiter and in identifying the fate of Rome with the divine purpose and will he made the mythological creed discharge a true and important function in the poem, and in fact its only function; except for this, Olympus is only a traditional adornment, a part of the mechanical scheme and surface pictorialness of the plot, and one element in that many-sided perspective of human history in which the poem is so remarkably beyond all others. If, however, Olympus is a shadow and Virgil recedes from it in his mind, on the other hand he is far advanced and moves forward in what was to Homer the shadow-world, the life beyond the grave; in his thought and sentiment there is not only the sense of profound reality, but he touches on the confines of revealed religion. Here most strikingly, in the sweep backward to the still visible but fading gods and in the sweep forward to the still unborn Christian ages, the *Æneid* shows that characteristic of greatness in literature which lies in its being a water-shed of time; it looks back to antiquity in all that clothes it with the past of imagination, character and event, and forward to Christian times in all that clothes it with emotion, sentiment and finality to the heart. If, as is sometimes said, Gibbon's history is the bridge between the ancient and the modern world, the *Æneid* is the high central ridge where time itself joined both.

Virgil was so great a poet because he assimilated his vast mental experience, and turned it, in the true Roman way, to power over the future. His language itself—and he was the "lord of language" —bears the Roman stamp. Scarce any poet is so brief; like all the masters of poetic speech he seldom carries his sentence beyond three lines, and more often he clasps the sense in shorter limits, and notably in those "half-lines" which are so often spoken of as the special characteristic of his style, though they are also to be found in Shakespeare with like power. Oratory belongs to the epic as the lyric belongs to the drama, as its rhetorical means of intensity; and oratory was a Roman art. It belongs to Virgil equally with his winged music. It is the oratory of Brutus, not of Antony; and it is present in spirit and method, not only in the set speeches and narratives, but in the general flow of the verse; the weight of thought, the compactness of vision, the intensity of the lyrical cry of feeling itself, are indebted to it, for it is the native world of Roman speech, and Virgil in his song could only heighten, refine and amplify it, pour it in more lucid and tender voices of the spirit, which was none the less a Roman spirit. It is common to regard the earlier books of the *Æneid* which are more inspired by the Greek element in Virgil's culture as the greater; but in the later books in which the inspiration of the home-land prevails more, and not less excellently in its own qualities, if the presence of Rome is less imperially impressive, it has more primitive charm. The early air of Rome is here, the youth of primeval Italy, when Empire was far away. In Mezentius and Turnus, and especially in Evander, there is an original impulse, a native stamp; and, most of all, in Camilla. Few poets cast a new type of womanhood. Camilla is the first of those ideal Italian women who have glorified the pages of Tasso and the canvasses, divine and human, of a hundred artists. If the later books of the *Æneid* are less valued, it is partly because they are purer in originality, more Italian in their interest, and in limiting themselves to the evolution of a romantic past for the soil of Italy and the beginnings of Rome make a narrower appeal. To Virgil this task was, perhaps, dearer than the echoes of Troy and the sorrows of Carthage, but he worked with names that sounded less in the ears of the world. In one respect he succeeds marvelously; both on the voyage and in Italy he gives the sense of the early Mediterranean world as a place of wandering colonists and rising settlements in lonely places, a sense of the taking possession of the virgin land, with seas and coasts and spaces never to be crossed again; such a wonder-world did not come to man's view a second time, so effectually, till the days of Cortez and Magellan and De Soto, in the dawn of the Americas. The primitive time, such as it is shown in Evander, has the same reality, and his hospitality has retained in men's minds its place as the historic and ideal moment of the simplicities of the first life of men on still unviolated soil. If one's eye is on the Roman spirit of the poem, he will not find the Italian prepossession of its last books an obstacle to his interest;

but rather the charm of a more home-bred inspiration will endear to him its humilities, its native character and the nobility of human feeling which is nowhere in the poem so constant, pervasive and pure. If Rome is less, in these passages, in her imperial form, Italy is more; and it is that Italy in which the true Rome resided and to which she returned, of which the Empire itself now seems a planet she cast from her larger and more immortal life.

The poem of Rome, however, even though such a nation as Italy fall heir to it, could not maintain its intimacy with the modern mind and continue to make a direct appeal to life, unless it were something more. There is a greatness in the *Æneid* beyond the presence of Rome in the verse. It might seem that Virgil was by nature little fitted for the epic; his initiation into life had been through that "passive youth" which Shelley describes, the type of poetic boyhood, sensitive, impressible, inexhaustibly recipient; and all his days he was a scholar drawing into his brooding thoughts the spectacle of things till his knowledge was equal to the world-culture of his time; that such a man should give back to the world what he had received from it in the shape of a poem of action seems incongruous, and, doubtless, like Tasso and Milton and Spenser and Tennyson, in their several degrees, he experienced the natural difficulties of the task. Yet, to the brooding spirit, not thought, but action is the true sphinx of life; not what is dreamed or reasoned or desired, but what is done, what God permits, as the phrase goes, the power of unrighteousness that is nine-tenths of life; this fastens the eye, perplexes the mind, disturbs the heart.

Virgil, born late and acquainted with the world long lived in, was of a contemplative mind; in the *Æneid* thought shadows every word, a subtle judgment blends with every action clothing it, as music clothes the line, in an element of its own, pitying, appealing, affirming, according to the motions of the poet's soul; and hence the *Æneid* has its grandest phase, by virtue of which it has entered into the hearts of so many later generations and still enters. It is a meditation upon life.

The modes in which the poem thus affects the reader are infinitely varied; sometimes so intimate as to seem the voice in one's own heart of one's own life, or so lofty and assured as to seem the voice of all men's hearts, or so world-sweeping in its pathos as to seem the voice divine. Unbroken is the sense of the difficulty of life, not merely under its old conception as a warfare, but as a thing of burden, of frequent mistake, of unforeseen and unmerited disaster, of repeated defeat, of uncertain issue; the toiling power of Rome is made up of the innumerable toils of miserable men, and about the main actors are the files of captive women, the sons burning on their funeral pyres before the faces of their parents, all the wretchedness of a military state for the private life. The element of difficulty felt in the reverses of the main fortune of the tale, in its birth in the terrors of the last night of Ilium, in the wrong landings, the insidious dangers of Carthage, the burning of the fleet, is, on the individual scale broken into a thousand cries of death and sorrow essentially personal and domestic. Life on land and sea is a field of battle, and everywhere are corpses rolled by Simois or the ocean-wave, and in every prospect the heart follows the remnant of men, in their beaten courage ever more courageous, but none the less victims of life. "Pain, pain, ever, forever," rings through the poem like a Promethean cry; the burden of Priam, the burden of Dido, the burden of Turnus, kingdom after kingdom, and by the way the strewn corpses of Palinurus, Euryalus, Pallas. In the Elysian fields Æneas marvels why any soul should desire to see the light of life. Over all there hangs in heaven the doubtful interest of the gods in human fates. "If any gods be just" —"if there be any kindness in heaven"— these are the refrains of all the prayers. In the presence of the mystery of what is done on earth the reason, always unsatisfied, will not be silent and refuses to yield its just share in the conduct of life; if, in one age, the tale be of Eden and the Fall, this offends the mind's sense of justice; if, in another time, it be of the struggle for existence from the dawn of life, this offends the mind's sense of mercy; in knowledge of justice and mercy, the mind finds its own superiority to the environment in which it is imprisoned, and in its moods of sincerest reason still seeks refuge in the provisional prayer on Virgil's lips.

Lucretius had lived; and something of all this difficulty, pain and uncertainty had come to light in that great intellect. He was essentially one of the eternal Puritan brood, personal revolters against church and state, which in history have been the twin tyrants of mankind; he looked back on the past and saw there immense and long-continued error in important parts of life, the delusion and woe of whole peoples since time began; and he denounced superstition as the mother of human ills. He was an individualist, a man of conscious virtue, self-sufficing; he had an empire in his mind; he spoke out, a lonely intellect in a world stripped for his eyes to the bare principles of its being and in his words was the fiery seed of the new universe of scientific thought. Virgil was of a different strain, a natural worshiper, reverent of the rite, attached to the myth, clinging with his affections to the outward garniture of life and history; but his eyes were on the same things that Lucretius saw. He, too, was finding in philosophy the true goal. He felt from youth the compelling power of thought of Rome's greatest mind as he looked out on the long Pagan retrospect of life's beauty and sorrow. How did he save himself from the intellectual indignation, the despair of the divine, the earthly pessimism of Rome's great sceptic; for the face of Virgil, "majestic in his sadness at the doubtful doom of human kind," is the grave face of a believer. He saved himself by the power of love.

He was a lover of life; only an immense love of life could have so revealed to him the pity of it. At every touch he shows a spirit naturally dependent; teachable, yielding, hospitable, responsive, sympathetic, appealing, his heart flows out upon things, uniting with them at every contact, from his early loves of nature, romance and antiquity, his long passion of patriotism, on to his brooding over the fates of men; and yet with his self-surrender to the things of life there goes, equal with it, the true Roman self-control; it is a surrender that returns to him as strength. At every turn of the verse he evokes the moment of beauty from the natural world, and from life its moment of pain, with the clarity of the poet; charm, which is the one, and pathos, which is the other, are the words that leap from the heart in the memory of what he wrote, and after these the third is majesty, which is the principle of control in him, and completes and perfects his genius. These are wonderfully softened by his constant tenderness. The epics generally find no place for children in them; but here there are three—Astyanax, Ascanius and Marcellus—and two of these are dead boys. Of all Virgil's loves, the greatest in power is the love of human life; and it is this that makes the poem so Christian-like, because it is embodied and conveyed in the forms of sorrow and especially of bereavement. Yet the burden of that sorrow comes as the burden of the Roman world running its long career of battle-strife; here is the heart of Rome beating in the only Roman breast in which it had become fully conscious of itself. The world was ready to be re-born; there is no break; the premonitions of Christian feeling are natural to Virgil. It is this that makes him of all ancient writers the nearest to modern times, of all epic poets the nearest to all nations. The *Æneid* is, I think, the greatest single book written by man because of its inclusiveness of human life, of life long lived, in the things of life. It is the dirge of Rome; majestic in its theme, beautiful in its emotions, sad in its philosophy, it is almost the dirge of life; yet many a modern mind still turns from the contemplation of human life in history, like the thousands of old days, to Virgil, and says with Dante, *Tu se' lo mio maestro,* "Thou art my master."

*Of this book, eleven hundred copies were made for the members of
The Authors Club and for presentation to scholarly institutions*

M C M      X X X

*The Pynson Printers of New York*

La Bibliothèque                    The Lib
vers   d'                   a